Little Pebble™

Our Pets

Fish

by Lisa J. Amstutz

raintree

a Capstone company — publishers for children

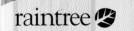

Raintree is an imprint of Capstone Global Library Limited, a company incorporated in England and Wales having its registered office at 264 Banbury Road, Oxford, OX2 7DY – Registered company number: 6695582

www.raintree.co.uk
myorders@raintree.co.uk

Edited by Marissa Kirkman
Designed by Juliette Peters (cover) and Charmaine Whitman (interior)
Picture research by Morgan Walters
Production by Laura Manthe
Originated by Capstone Global Library Limited
Printed and bound in India

ISBN 978 1 4747 5717 1 (hardback)
22 21 20 19 18
10 9 8 7 6 5 4 3 2 1

ISBN 978 1 4747 5430 9 (paperback)
23 22 21 20 19 18
10 9 8 7 6 5 4 3 2 1

British Library Cataloguing in Publication Data
A full catalogue record for this book is available from the British Library.

Acknowledgements
We would like to thank the following for permission to reproduce photographs: Alamy: Ammit, 17; Newscom: Solent News/Splash News, 21; Shutterstock: Ammit Jack, top 9, Baronb, bottom 11, bluehand, middle right back cover, chaythawin, middle left back cover, Dmitry Sheremeta, bottom 15, Eric Isselee, left back cover, fivespots, right back cover, Galina Savina, top 11, Kanticha Panichkul, 5, Kletr, middle back cover, luckypic, bottom 19, MAT, top 15, Mirek Kijewski, Cover, bottom 7, bottom 9, Mirko Rosenau, top left back cover, Mr Aesthetics, (wood) design element throughout, MrZeroman, top 7, Napat, 13, Panupon Eurawong, top 19, Tretyakov Viktor, 1

Every effort has been made to contact copyright holders of material reproduced in this book. Any omissions will be rectified in subsequent printings if notice is given to the publisher.

All the Internet addresses (URLs) given in this book were valid at the time of going to press. However, due to the dynamic nature of the Internet, some addresses may have changed, or sites may have changed or ceased to exist since publication. While the author and publisher regret any inconvenience this may cause readers, no responsibility for any such changes can be accepted by either the author or the publisher.

Contents

Look!

A bright fish swims

to the top of its tank.

Gulp!

It eats a treat.

All about fish

Pet fish can be big or small.

They can be any colour.

Some are as clear as glass!

A fish can breathe in water.

It opens its mouth.

It pumps water through

its gills.

gills

Zip! A fish swims quickly.

Its tail pushes it along.

Fins help it steer.

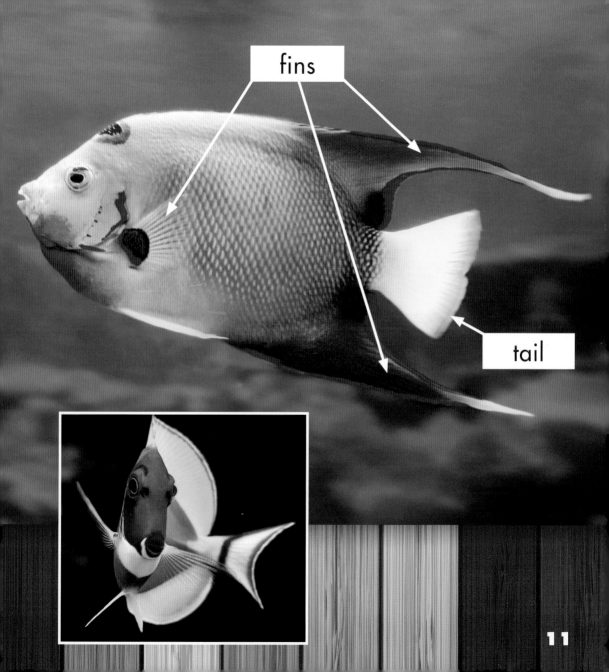

fins

tail

Most pet fish have scales.

They are hard and clear.

Pet fish eat fish food.

It comes in flakes or pellets.

Some fish eat plants too.

Growing up

Some fish lay eggs.

Other fish give birth to young.

Fish babies are called fry.

fry

Fish often live in groups.

Sometimes they chase
each other.

Zoom!

Play time

This fish does tricks.

It swims through a hoop.

It chases a toy.

Fish are fun pets!

Glossary

chase   to follow something quickly

fin   body part that fish use to swim and steer in water

flake   small, flat piece of something; some fish food comes in flakes

fry   young fish

gill   body part on the side of a fish; fish use their gills to breathe

pellet   small, hard piece of food

scale   one of the small pieces of hard skin covering the body of a fish

steer   to move in a certain direction

tank   container that holds water

Read more

Goldie's Guide to Caring for Your Goldfish (Pets' Guides), Anita Ganeri (Raintree, 2014)

How to Look After Your Goldfish: A Practical Guide to Caring For Your Pet, In Step-By-Step Photographs, David Alderton (Armadillo Books, 2013)

Pet Fish: Questions and Answers (Pet Questions and Answers), Christina Mia Gardeski (Capstone Press, 2017)

Websites

www.bbc.co.uk/cbeebies/topics/pets
Discover a variety of pets, play pet games and watch pet videos on this fun BBC website.

www.bluecross.org.uk
Find out more about how to choose a pet and care for your pet on the Blue Cross website.

Comprehension questions

1. What do pet fish eat?

2. What body parts help fish swim?

3. How do fish breathe?

Index